Copyrights   2012 by Woodroe C. Nicholson
All rights reserved. No part of this publication may be
reproduced, stored, in retrieval system, or transmitted in
any form or by any means, electronic, mechanical, photo
copying, recording or otherwise, without the prior written
permission of the publisher.

Canadian Cataloging in Publication Data

Nicholson, Woodroe
GOLF FOR EVERY <u>BODY</u>
ISBN 978-0-9682885-4-2

Cover design and graphics by Woodroe C. Nicholson
Printed and bound in Canada by:

Sawbuck Ventures Ltd.
RR3 2225 Northey's Road
Lakefield, ON K0L 2H0

NOTE:

Originally this instruction book was my golf diary, it slowly evolved as I kept notes during my long journey back to playing golf after a hip injury. I never intended to publish it.

I'm not a professional golfer; my golfing friends and others I have taught encouraged me to publish this book, but it took a stranger playing in our foursome to convince me. After we had played a few holes I complimented him on his swing; he told me that he was a beginner. To my surprise he held up a few pages of my golf notes that I had given to our mutual friend. After I informed him that they were from my golf diary, he asked if he could have a copy and suggested I should consider writing a golf instruction book. This is it. I hope it helps you as much as it helped him and others.

Acknowledgment

A Special Thanks To Ron Morris

I was fortunate enough to meet or play with some of Canada's best touring pros during the late sixties and early seventies. Ron Morris, my wife Diane's uncle, was the head teaching professional at Whiteville Golf and Country Club, located near Toronto, Ontario. Ron and other golfers such as Moe Norman, Al Balding, George Knudson and other professionals played in a few tournaments at my club, Uplands Golf and Country Club. I learned a lot from them.

Ron not only helped me with my game, he was kind enough to let me play practice rounds with he and Moe during the winter months; they played what they called "the Florida Grape Fruit League." I never forgot those early lessons. As I was re-learning my swing, it reminded me of just how much he had taught me.

Thanks uncle Ron.

37. BACKSWING CHECKS
    Checking your backswing

39. THE DOWNSWING
    Plant your left foot
    Your lower body leads
    Wrists release just before impact
    The momentum continues

45. THE FINISH
    Check your finish during practice
    Bad balance
    The downswing moves

49. YOUR PRE-SWING TEMPO

49. PRE-SWING WAGGLE

50. PRACTICE WITHOUT THE BALL

51 PRACTICING WITH THE BALL
    Why and how the ball fades etc.
    A hinged wrist fundamental
    Don't stare after ball contact
    Think "swing", " not hit"
    The problem isn't too much right hand
    Feel the left arm leading the right
    Forget distance and direction
    Not trusting your swing

8. GOLF FOR EVERY <u>BODY</u>

2. YOUR BODY'S NATURAL SWING

15. THE GRIP
      A correct grip is a must
      Soling the club
      Neutral left hand grip
      Left hand grip check
      Neutral right hand grip
      Grip pressure

21. YOUR HEAD MOVES ON ITS OWN

22. TENSION VERSES POWER

22. THE BACKSWING KEYS
      For every action there's a reaction

26. THE STANCE
      Side view
      Right foot supports the backswing

29. BRUSH THE GRASS

32. THE BACKSWING
      Brush the grass
      Arms follow the left side
      Wrists hinge on their own
      Feel the weight over your right foot

57. IRON CLUBS

58. THE SHORT GAME
    Half shots or less
    Three quarter shots
    Feeling the distance

62. CHIPPING
    Setting up to the ball
    Hand finish ahead of the ball
    Chipping practice
    Further the distance, shorter the club
    Between fifteen and five feet
    Between thirty and fifteen feet
    Good chipping relieves tension

68. THE WEDGE LOB SHOT

70. THE IRON LOW PUNCH SHOT

71. SAND SHOTS

72. PUTTING
    The backswing
    The follow through

76. DRIVER, 3-WOOD AND
    UTILITY CLUBS

77. PROBLEMS ON THE COURSE

Stretch before playing or practicing
Warm up without a ball first
Don't keep score for at least five rounds
The practice swing first
Controlling your ego
On thinking positive
Focus where you want the ball to land
Swing and go look for it
Ignore your butterflies
Practice creates confidence

85. TEACHING NOTES
Swinging over the top
Skipping the practice swing
Not completing the shoulder turn
Hitting at the ball
Stiff arms and too far from the ball
Slowing to watch the ball
Hands closing the club face

90. SWING CURES
Trust your swing
Keep notes after every round

95. FINAL WORDS

GOLF FOR EVERY BODY

I began playing golf in my twenties. When I was forty-four I injured my left hip while playing tennis. I had to give up all the sports I loved, golf, tennis and running. The doctors wouldn't do a hip replacement, they told me I was too young and could still manage to walk, I would have to wait. I waited for ten years.

Finally at age fifty-five they replaced the bad hip. Ten days after the operation. I was released from the hospital on crutches. My hip just didn't feel right, something was wrong. I didn't know what was wrong until I went for my first check up a few weeks later. The doctor informed me my leg was an inch shorter than my right leg; my left hip wouldn't turn fully and my foot was turned out at least 30 degrees to the left. At first I was in shock; for a while I was depressed.

I knew running was out and tennis was out, but I thought I could still play golf, my favorite sport. As soon as I attempted to swing a club I discovered I couldn't: my hips wouldn't turn far enough during my downswing, which caused the club to swing out over the top (outside to in). When my feet faced the target line, most of my weight was on my short left leg, which kept me off balance, and my hips and shoulders were closed. When I added a one inch lift to my left shoe, it raised my knee an inch higher than my right, this encouraged my body to come up out of the swing.

One afternoon while I was experimenting with the possibility of swinging a club left handed (my right hip could turn further during the downswing), a long time golfing buddy discreetly pointed to a one legged golfer about to tee off. He was standing up balancing on his one leg. We watched as he waggled the club, then hit the ball into the middle of the fairway at least 200 yards. Afterwards, he hopped back to the cart, waved and took off down the course. I was truly inspired, I was convinced I could re-learn the golf swing. If he could play golf so could I. And so began my long journey back to golf. I knew there had to be a way for me to solve the hip and leg problems.

I decided to become my own instructor. " I was the only one who really knew and understood the obstacles I had to overcome." I began reading all the personal golf notes I had written to myself over the years. I even looked at some of my old score cards to remind me that I was once a better than average golfer. I watched the golf professionals on the weekends and listened to the commentators as they analyzed, then explained the good and bad swings. I read everything about golf I could get my hands on.

My journey lasted three years. I experimented with every bit of this information and a few golf gimmicks as well. I would analyze it first then swing a club either indoors or outdoors depending on the weather. If I liked what it was doing for my swing, I practiced with a ball. Because I live in a rural area close to a hay field, I hit as many balls as I needed to. I hit thousands. Even during the winter, when I could find a small patch of green I practiced outdoors. I kept a golf club in my bedroom to practice in a mirror, on whatever I was currently working on, before turning out the lights.

When spring arrived each year, I took my swing to the golf course to put it to the test. Often when I was experimenting at the practice range the golf instructor would look over. He seemed to be asking, " do you want some help." Even though I had already experienced many disappointments, I didn't. Whenever I considered giving up, I would recall the one legged golfer.

It wasn't until the third winter that I felt confident my swing would hold up on the golf course. I continued swinging the club indoors, impatiently waiting for a patch of green to arrive. When it finally did, I went outdoors, dropped a few balls onto the patch and swung. I knew I had found my swing, but I had to wait a few more weeks for the practice range to open to confirm it. Three weeks later I did. My new swing hadn't deserted me.

I can honestly say that I am a better golfer than I ever was, not just because my swing is better than it was, I have learned to approach the game differently. I know why I play it; this may sound corny to some; my soul needs the inner peace, I need the life lessons and the personal satisfaction.

I've never met the one legged golfer, I don't even know his name. If I could, I would thank him from the bottom of my heart. He taught me the best golf lessen of all: you may have to make a few adjustments, but golf is for every <u>body</u>. Every body has a natural swing, discover yours.

Woodroe C. Nicholson

YOUR BODY'S NATURAL SWING

Knowing and understanding your swing builds confidence, creates positive thinking, and gets good results. Not knowing where the clubhead should be during the swing, how to get it there, or when it should be there, makes golfers anxious and creates tension. Once you've learned how to teach your body a few tried, proven and easy to do swing keys, the other moves will happen naturally. You won't need to spend months learning by trial and error. You'll also be able to detect a swing problem on your own and correct it, instead of grooving it into a bad habit, sometimes even while on the golf course.

Most beginner golfers know what a good golf swing looks like, they've seen the best golfers in the world on television and in golf magazines. They may even have watched all the positions in slow motion. However, when they attempt to learn the game, they soon discover it's difficult to organize all the necessary moving parts to send the ball in the right direction. Just because they can recognize good golf swings, it doesn't mean they understand the process any more than if they were to watch a magician do a trick could they perform it. They must understand the fundamentals of the golf swing; more importantly, they must learn how to practice them. Personal video cameras show golfers what's wrong with their swing, but not why or how to fix it.

I won't tell you about all the golf theories and gimmicks I tried, too much information is as bad as not enough, it ties your mind and body up in knots. No golfer can think of all those swing positions at once and get good results while he or she is actually playing golf. Maybe you've heard the story about the octopus: Someone once asked him which one of his tentacles did his body move first. After he thought about it for a while, he replied, " I don't know." Then he tried to move, but couldn't he was paralyzed!

My instructions are organized in sequence and illustrated with swing key photos to show and teach you how to develop a reliable golf swing and short game. Soon you'll also be able to detect, analyze and correct a swing problem on your own.

Before you begin to learn how to teach your body the swing keys, you must first learn to grip the club and set up to the ball correctly, and understand the difference between tension and power. Your new swing depends on how well you learn these fundamentals.

To begin learning you don't have to go to a practice range. It's easier at first and more beneficial to learn without a ball, in your backyard. For the benefit of the beginner golfer, I have purposely re-frained from using a lot of golf jargon.

Okay, let's get started

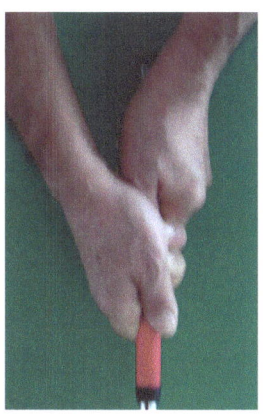

THE GRIP
A correct grip is a must

During your swing, your hands subconsciously return to their neutral position; if you don't place your grip on the club correctly, the clubface will be either open or closed at impact. Consequently you will develop numerous swing errors, because your body naturally tries in some unorthodox manner, to compensate for the incorrect grip.

Some golfers try to solve their swing problems with a weak or strong grip, when really they should be looking for the swing problem. Compensating for a bad swing with the wrong grip only ingrains the problem.

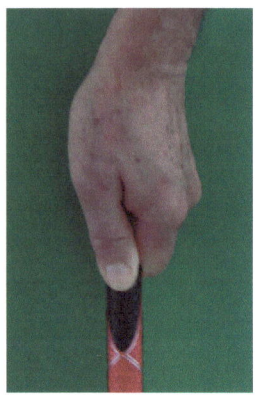

Soling the club

To assist you in soling the club correctly, most golf grips have a large or small mark on the top. The clubface is square if this mark is positioned in the center of the grip (as shown above).

Set up with the ball placed just inside your left heel. With your right hand, sole the club behind the ball and square the bottom of the club face on an imaginary straight line to a target. Maintain the club's natural soled position: as explained earlier, during the downswing your hands will return the clubface to its original soled position.

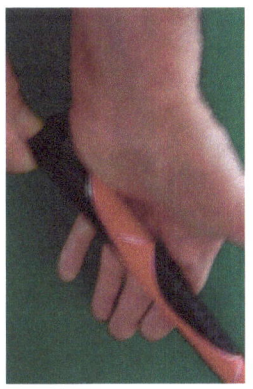

Neutral Left hand grip

Hold the club with your right hand forefinger and thumb while you place your left grip onto the club. Without moving the club face, open your left hand and place the shaft's grip across the base of your forefinger and position the fleshy pad (above your baby finger) on top of the grip, as shown.

Close the fingers against the fleshy pad and push the club's grip up into it. Next fold your thumb, it fits centered naturally on top of the shaft. You should see your two top knuckles. Your palm and all your fingers secure the club throughout the swing.

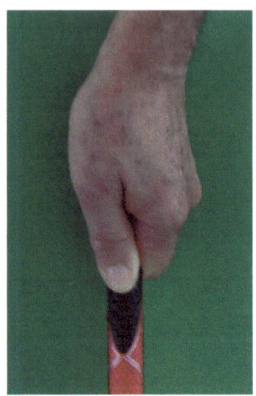

Left Hand Grip Check

With your left hand, lift your club up about a foot out in front of you. Remove three fingers from the club: your middle finger, third finger and baby finger. If your grip is positioned correctly, your forefinger and the fleshy pad above your baby finger will secure the club

    Some experienced golfers square the clubface and place the shaft against the base of their left hand's forefinger and below its fleshy pad; they close their forefinger and lift the club up; press their fingers upwards and place their thumb on top of the shaft.

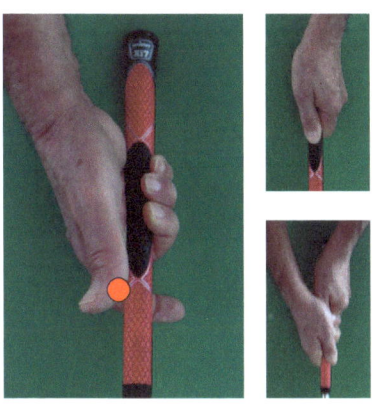

Neutral Right hand grip

Your right hand grip is a finger grip. Your left hand grip holds the clubface steady while you position your right hand. With your opened right hand relaxed and hanging down, place it against the club. The shaft's grip lies across the base of your fingers: below the palm. Curl your index, third and middle fingers around it; your right thumb nestles comfortably on top of your left thumb and your right palm fits snug against the back of your left hand.

Curl your baby finger around your left index finger or you may interlock your left index finger with your right baby finger (whatever feels the most comfortable).

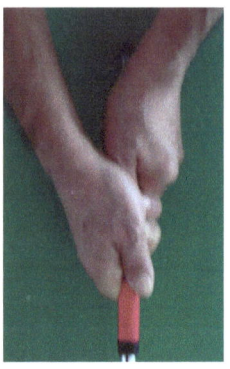

Grip Pressure

Tight grips destroy good swings; when your grip pressure is tight, instead of just firm, your whole body becomes tense, especially your forearms. Sometimes tight grips prevent your right elbow from folding correctly at the top of your backswing. Your grip must be just firm enough to secure the club from the beginning of your backswing until you complete your follow-through.

      To establish your natural grip pressure: relax your arms and sole the club; lift it up above your waist without consciously increasing your grip pressure. Waggle the club back and forth; you should feel the clubhead. Notice, if additional grip pressure was required, it has increased without you thinking about it.

THE HEAD MOVES ON IT'S OWN

" The best way to think about your head is don't: during the swing it will move on it's own, and prior to ball contact it will remain still on it's own."

How many times have heard someone tell another golfer to keep his or her head still. Bad advice.

Try this simple experiment: Keep your head perfectly still; swing a golf club backwards as high as your head and forwards as high as your head. Notice it's impossible to do. Now allow your head to move on it's own; swing the club backwards and forwards as far as you can. Notice how freely your arms move as your weight naturally transfers from one foot to the other. During the forward motion your head and chest turned to face forward and your right heel may have come up. All this occurred because your head wasn't constricting your body.

Convinced? The only difference between this and your actual golf swing is your head remains still at impact. The most important thing for you to remember is: prior to the bottom of your downswing your head doesn't remain still and you should not interfere with it. During the backswing it moves backwards a few inches, it may even move further back just prior to impact.

After impact your head moves forward so your body can transfer most of your weight onto your left leg.

TENSION vs POWER

Tension is necessary in a golf swing. What you don't want is your arms attempting to muscle the ball to create power. If your big arm muscles take over the swing they'll destroy your tempo and your swing.

I hear many golfers telling their buddies "slow your swing, you're swinging too fast." They should be telling them to learn to swing with their entire body instead of just muscling the ball with their forearms.

THE BACKSWING KEYS

Hitting away at golf balls for hours to learn how to swing a golf club correctly, or to solve an unknown backswing problem by experimenting with golf tips you don't understand traps you in a vicious circle. Usually it destroys your chances of developing a good swing. You must practice with a purpose, if you don't know what you're trying to learn or correct, you're teaching your body an unreliable swing. It may work for awhile, but like a house on a poor foundation, it won't hold up for long. Take your time and build a sound swing, brick by brick.

Before you begin to practice the three backswing keys, you must first understand the importance of your stance (setting up to the ball correctly), keeping your body level and the right foot anchor (pages 26-31).

Practice these three keys to discover your natural golf swing. You may experience some bumps along the way, but don't look for shortcuts or take detours, or you won't achieve your goal. Later, when your swing gets off track, and it will, even professional golfers experience bad swing days, you'll be able to refer to these three keys to get back on track.

Set up to the club with your upper arms hanging down as passive as a soft rope, you don't want a tight grip, or tension in your arms. Your neutral grip should feel as one unit; however, only your left hand controls the club, your right hand just moves along with the club for now.

1) Your hands and arms don't lift the club up off the grass on their own. "Your entire left side (as one unit) turns around to the right; your hands, arms, knees, hips and shoulders push the club back brushing the grass along the target line, then inside the line until the club lifts off the grass."

2) When your arms and the club shaft are parallel to the surface, the back of your left hand will be facing outwards, the arms, wrists and club shaft will form a straight line parallel to the target line. The wrists won't be hinged yet.

During practice you can check the first position before swinging the club back: place a club shaft or a yard stick on the surface, along the front of your feet, parallel to the target line.

3) The left arm, wrists and shaft maintain this in line position as your left side continues turning to lift the club. The wrists, if they are relaxed, begin to hinge on their own; they remain in a straight line with the arms and shaft as they travel to the top of the backswing.

After your left side completes the turn and lifts the club to the top of your backswing, your weight will be positioned mostly over your right foot, your left shoulder will be turned behind the ball and the club will be pointed over your right shoulder with the clubshaft parallel to your target line.

They're not difficult moves, but some

beginners either can't or don't complete their backswing. Usually it's because they don't allow their head to move back far enough to transfer most of their body's weight over their right foot. This problem usually occurs when their hands take over from their left side to swing the club to the top.

Practice these three backswing positions until the club is parallel at the top, they must be correct before beginning to practice the downswing.

For every action there's a reaction

Your body's left side, as one unit (arm, knee, hip and shoulder): turned into your right leg, turned your right hip rearwards, moved your head and shifted most of your weight onto your right foot, folded your right elbow at the top of your backswing and your wrists are hinged. You should be aware of these moves, but don't attempt to control them individually.

THE STANCE

The stance width varies: it should be wide enough for good balance, but not wider than your hips; the shorter the club the narrower the stance. Distribute your weight evenly between your feet. Bend your knees; sit down slightly. Notice because your right hand is below your left hand, your shoulders are tilted and your head is positioned behind the ball. *continued...*

Side view

Let your hands hang like a soft rope. Grip the club and lift it up in front of you, about parallel to the grass; let the club drop; bend forward just far enough to sole the bottom edge of the clubface square to the target line.   If your hands and arms don't interfere as you lower the club to the grass, they will be positioned the correct distance from your body and the clubface will be in the correct position to brush the grass or to contact the ball at impact.

Right foot supports the backswing

During your backswing the right hip turns rearward; your right foot supports the weight that's being distributed over to your right hip. At the top of your swing you should feel that most of your weight is being supported by your right leg and foot: you don't want your weight to get outside of your right foot (past it). When your left side turns the club back, your head on it's own, moves back towards your right foot. Your legs should feel responsive but relaxed.

BRUSH THE GRASS
to learn your swing

Some golfers may have told you that your bad swing is the result of one or all of the following swing errors: your body moves up off the ball; you're lifting the club up with just your hands; you're swinging the club around over the top during the downswing. This is the tail wagging the dog: it's because you're not swinging the club in the correct sequence. You can solve these and other swing problems from the ground up. I did and so can you, regardless of your body's condition, shape or size.

Brushing the clubhead along the grass as you begin to turn your left side, and brushing it again through the impact zone subconsciously trains your body to swing correctly; it also keeps you from trying to control all the moves your body has to make during your swing, and it compensates for most body limitations. After brushing the grass, during my practice swing, I have only one backswing thought, "turn my left side." If you want a shortcut to developing a reliable backswing and get good results faster than most, this is it. Forget the ball for now, teach your body to swing the club: practice turning your left side to brush the club back and through the grass. Later, when you're on the golf course, you should continue to brush it before the actual swing.

For example, you can solve the popular downswing problem even seasoned golfers are always talking about, "swinging their right shoulder around over the top; it should be turning down under their left shoulder through the impact area." If you practice brushing the grass before every golf shot you shouldn't have this problem:

the club can't brush the grass through the impact zone unless your right shoulder moves downwards far enough to reach it; your body subconsciously moves correctly.

Before I began to practice brushing the grass I couldn't get my body to adjust to the one inch lift on my left shoe; it lifted my left knee an inch higher than my right knee: my body moved up at impact and I would miss-hit the ball. My left hip wouldn't turn fully either. I tried everything I could think of to solve these problems, nothing worked. I had to practice for a few weeks before I could brush the club back and through the grass; when I could, I solved these problems. I also discovered I was no longer swinging the club around over the top.

My old swing is back. Now as long as I program my body by brushing the grass before every golf shot, my swing is usually good.

THE BACKSWING
Practice without a ball first!

First set up beside the ball (or to brush where the ball would be) with your arms hanging down as passive as a soft rope. Place the club facing the target line. Your left hand secures the club; your right hand doesn't, it just travels along with the club, later it helps to support it.

1) Brush the grass

Move your entire left side: your hands, arms, knees, hips and shoulders as one unit, push the club back along the grass. The club will turn inside the target line just before it's lifted off the grass. Your hands and arms do not lift the club on their own. You should feel that some of your left sides weight is being transferred to your right foot, be sure not to let it move to the outside of your right foot.

2) Arms follow your left side

When your arms and the clubshaft are at or close to parallel to the surface, the back of your left hand will be facing outwards; the arms, wrists and clubshaft will form a straight line parallel to the target line. The wrists won't be hinged yet.

During practice: place a club or yard stick parallel to the target line (shown here). If your arms didn't interfere with the turning of your left side, the club is parallel to the target line. If it isn't, your right hand may be controlling it.

Wrists hinge on their own

Continue turning your left side to turn and lift the club further around and upwards: Your right leg will be positioned over your right foot and your head will move further backwards as your shoulders turn. Your left arm, wrists and the shaft are still in the inline position and your wrists are hinging on their own; they will remain in this straight line as they travel to the top of your back-swing.

3) Feel the weight over your right foot

Your left side continued turning to complete your backswing: your weight is positioned over your right foot; your left shoulder is turned behind the ball; the clubshaft is over your right shoulder, pointing in a straight line parallel to your target line; the wrists are hinged; your right elbow is pointing downward; the left knee is turned toward your right knee; the right hip is turned rearward to the right.

BACKSWING CHECKS

With your back facing a large mirror or your reflection in an outside window, turn your left side to brush the grass.

continued...

Checking your backswing

Set up with your back facing a large mirror or facing your reflection in an outside window. Turn your left side as a unit to brush the grass before it begins lifting the club to the top.

If your practice backswing was correct at the top of the swing, your weight is over your right foot; the clubshaft is parallel to the target line and positioned over the your right shoulder; your left shoulder is behind the ball; your right elbow is pointing downward; your wrists are hinged; your left knee is pointing to your right knee; your right hip is turned rearward to the right.

If your arms aren't parallel to the target line, chcck the first position with a yard stick: if they just lifted the club up instead of turning as a unit with your left side the club won't be parallel to the target line at the top.

Trust your new backswing as your body learns these positions. Other than your left arm pushing the club back as it turns as a unit with your left side; don't attempt to control your swing, just feel it. The more you practice the sooner your body will be able to perform these moves as one: just by turning your left side.

THE DOWNSWING

Your head doesn't move forward until after impact. Start your downswing smoothly: it's important not to jerk the club down with your hands, if you do you'll destroy your swing. Plant your left foot first: your left knee will straighten some; your hips will slide forward and turn towards your left leg, the anchor. Your shoulders will follow along, turning and pulling your arms and hands down as one unit; your left shoulder will move upwards and your right shoulder will move downwards; your left arm will be straight and your bent right elbow will be brushing your right side. Your weight will be evenly distributed. Your hinged wrists and your hands will be approximately even with your waist; ready to release the clubhead into the impact zone.

From this point on you won't have conscious control of your swing: the energy that your backswing has created will propel the clubhead through the impact zone and release your hinged wrists; your left shoulder will continue moving upwards and your right shoulder will continue moving downwards to brush the grass. "You couldn't have stopped your wrists from releasing even if you wanted too."

During play, this energy propels the club through the impact zone to launch the ball to the target; it's momentum carries your hands and arms to the finish.

You only have to practice this one downswing move, the rest happens as soon as you plant your left foot: During practice, set up beside the ball and swing the club, focusing on brushing the grass back and though the impact zone. You will be programming your swing as you swing the club.

NOTE: If you can't brush the grass, your body isn't moving correctly, especially your lower body. You probably wouldn't be able make solid contact with the ball either.

There's more than one way to start the club downwards. However, I recommend planting your left foot first: as far as I am concerned it makes it much easier for your body to swing in the correct sequence. Other than planting my left foot, I don't consciously control my swing. Whatever downswing move you decide on, you must be able to brush the grass or none of them will work satisfactorily.

Plant your left foot

Your head doesn't move forward until after impact. Plant your left foot first; your hips will slide forward and turn towards your left leg, the anchor. Your shoulders will follow along to turn and pull your arms and hands down as one unit; the club will follow your shoulders, arms and the hinged wrists. Your hips and lower body continue moving.

Your lower body leads

Your left knee will straighten some. Your right elbow will be close to your right side, the left shoulder will be turned upwards and the right shoulder will be turned downwards, placing your arms on an inside path. Your weight will be evenly distributed between your feet. Your hinged wrists and your hands will be approximately even with your waist, ready to release the clubhead. From this point on you won't have conscious control of your swing!

Wrists release just before impact

Your upper body remains behind the ball. The stored up energy and the weight of the clubhead will propel your arms: forcing your hinged wrists to release the clubhead as it travels through the impact area. It will feel almost as if someone else has taken control of your swing. You couldn't have stopped your arms, or prevented your wrists from releasing the clubhead even if you had wanted too. "During practice swings only: brush the grass along the target line as far as possible."

The momentum continues

Your conscious work was over the moment you planted your left foot to release the energy, but its momentum will continue until it lifts your hands to finish at the top. In fact, the clubhead's speed through the impact zone moves too fast for a burst camera to catch it on film.

During actual play your results should have been good, if you brushed the grass correctly during your practice swing and you didn't attempt to control the club, especially through impact.

THE FINISH

REMINDER: Your head moves forward after ball contact to allow the momentum to continue as it moves your hands to the top of your downswing.

After your practice swing, your only swing thought should be "finish my swing." This will prevent your body from tensing up; it also prevents you from attempting to control the club through the impact area, or slowing your swing just before impact, destroying your tempo.

Check your finish during practice

If your head faces the target and your hands are hinged correctly, usually your swing is correct. This is because you focused on positioning your hands correctly at the top but you didn't consciously attempt to control them.

To check your finish: hold your hinged wrists position, turn your chest parallel to the target line, then lower your arms and hands to the surface; the clubface should be square, not closed or open.

Bad balance

Balance tells you a lot about your swing. If your tempo is too fast you'll know it: you won't be able stay in balance or maintain your finish. However, if your swing lacks momentum your body usually won't stay balanced either: you'll be lunging at the ball trying to get it air born. Balance and tempo, they depend on each other; when your body is in balance, sometimes it corrects small swing errors on it's own.

THE DOWNSWING MOVES

PRE-SWING TEMPO

Tempo is just as important as a good swing. Bad tempos destroy perfectly good swings; for example you will get into trouble if your arms move faster than your lower body. Golfers swing tempos vary: fast, slow, and in between.

Remember the one legged golfer I told you about, his tempo must have been good or he would have fallen over. You won't fall, but if your tempo is off, you will lose your balance and destroy your swing.

Every golfer has a natural swing tempo, you can discover yours. I don't know what it is but I can tell you how to discover it: maintain your balance while you swing the club until it makes a swishing sound that you can hear clearly. That's it, set up to the ball. Trust it, waggle the club and swing.

PRE-SWING WAGGLE

The pre-swing waggle is not an idle jester. Once you're set up over the ball waggle the club back and forth, mainly with your hands; your arms should be passive. Waggle the club briefly until you can feel the clubhead through your hands.

PRACTICE WITHOUT A BALL

Your goal is to learn a reliable golf swing, it's important at this stage to focus entirely on it, not the ball; select a mark on the grass to represent the ball. As explained earlier, during the downswing, brush the grass lightly with the club as it passes through the impact area.

Continue to monitor your backswing progress before and after every practice. You're your best teacher and critic. As explained previously, check the top of your backswing by placing your back in front of a mirror or an outside window's reflection. Do not attempt to practice with a ball until what you see is correct.

PRACTICING WITH A BALL

The swing positions shown on the previous pages were to help you understand each swing position. During actual play don't consciously try to perform them: you can't and you don't have too, "remember the octopus" They are the subconscious swing moves that you can expect after you have programmed your body's left side to co-ordinate the three swing keys into one smooth swing.

If your set-up is correct and you've practiced until you could turn your left side as one unit, the swing positions will happen automatically: you will have discovered what your body can do on it's own.

Why and how the ball fades, draws, slices, hooks, is pushed or pulled

FADE: Ball curves slightly to the right. The clubface was square at impact and the downswing came from outside the line.

DRAW: Ball curves slightly to the left. The clubface was square at impact and the downswing came from inside the line.

SLICE or PUSH: The ball curved or went on a straight line to the right. The clubface was open at impact and the club was on the target line.

PULL or HOOK: The ball curved or went on a straight line to the left. The clubface was closed at impact and the downswing came from outside the target line.

A hinged wrists fundamental

My son and I were on a practice range preparing for a round. He was swinging absolutely perfect. I was standing there watching him with pride when suddenly his perfect swing disappeared. He began to hook, slice and shank his long irons. I just watched. Totally exasperated, he finally asked for help. I suggested that he should relax his arms and grip to allow his wrists to hinge fully. His perfect swing returned.

Don't stare after ball contact

Some golfers heads get stuck over the ball after ball contact, blind golfers don't. Once a blind golfer knows where the ball is positioned he or she must trust their head to move when it should. Some sighted golfers slow their swing instead of allowing their head to move after ball contact, they fixate on where the ball was. Consequently, their swing doesn't have enough momentum to propel the clubhead to the finish.

I recall years ago, flailing away at balls trying to correct my swing. A good friend came over to me and said "you lied to your wife: you told her you were going to practice your swing today." I told him I was. He said, "no you're not, you're staring at golf balls." I told him I had to focus on the ball to hit it. He said, "no you don't, try shutting your eyes and swing." He was absolutely correct, my swing smoothed out and the ball contact was solid.

Try it: Ask a friend to watch the ball flight, while you close your eyes and swing. You'll be convinced.

Think "swing", not "hit"

Good results depend on a smooth, repeatable swing. It's very important to think "swing" and "tempo", not "hit", as you practice "Golf For Every Body".

This is why I teach the swing without a ball first. When you think about it, the ball has to move, it's in the middle of the swing path. Where it lands depends on your swing. This is not a chicken or egg situation; only a good swing consistently produces good results. Golf balls and clubs perform as the manufacturer intended, provided the swing is correct.

The problem isn't too much right hand

During your downswing your right hand instinctively comes into play on its own, about waist high. As long as your left hand continues to lead the clubhead it's almost impossible for the right hand to move too quickly through the ball.

Feel the left arm leading the right

Experience what it feels like to swing the club with the left hand leading the right. Place both hands on the grip, then take your right hand forefinger and thumb off of it, then swing the club. You can practice this with or without a ball.

Forget distance and direction

When you begin practicing with a ball, you'll be tempted to try the driver to see how far you can hit it. Don't. Practice with your three wood first, it's much easier to develop your swing with it because it's lighter than a driver. If you practice with your driver before you have grooved your swing, you may revert back to your old swing habits.

Don't be concerned about direction or you'll be tempted to control (steer) the clubhead. At this stage you should be learning to trust your swing. Tee the ball up. Set up to it facing towards a general direction with your shoulders parallel to your feet. Look at the landing area and swing.

Later, after you've grooved your swing and are practicing to a target, look for a mark in the grass in line with the target and the ball, about a foot in front of it. Aim the clubface at the mark. This aiming technique should be used in actual play as well.

Not trusting your swing

During my third summer back playing golf, I suddenly began to struggle with my swing. I tried every grip and swing key imaginable. Every once in a while I managed to play somewhat better, but my swing felt mechanical and tight. Not reliable, not even close. Even when I relaxed more it didn't help.

One afternoon, I was standing on the practice range totally puzzled, after another bad round of golf. I had just about finished off a large bucket of balls, so far the results were poor. While I was standing there mulling over the situation, I subconsciously began to swing my three iron back and forth. I noticed I could feel my body moving freely. It felt relaxed, especially my hands and wrists.

I decided to trust my body to swing the club. Without hesitating I stepped up to ball and swung. My swing was relaxed and powerful. The ball was right on target and my swing wasn't an effort. Ten perfect shots in a row. It was obvious that my practice swing was programming my body correctly, but I wasn't trusting it during actual play.

You may have noticed that some golfers practice swings are much better than their actual swing. This is usually because they really don't trust their swing on the golf course. Consequently they attempt to steer the ball. Their actual swing is usually faster as well. After your practice swing, your body is programmed to repeat it. Don't interfere with its natural flow. Trust it and swing.

    I'm not sure, but I think it was Ben Hogan, when asked, " who's the best swinger of a golf club? " He answered, "Probably some guy in Florida on a practice range." I think he was saying, "there's more pressure on the golf course, and that's where the game is played." You and I have seen professionals play really well three days in a row only to have a complete meltdown on the back nine on the final day. They didn't lose their swing, they lost trust in their swing. Trust and tension are both part of the game, the only way you can learn to handle tension and to practice trusting your swing is to play the game.

IRON CLUBS

Irons are designed to take a divot. Sole the bottom edge of the clubface behind the ball. Notice your hands are naturally ahead of the clubface, this is so the hands lead the clubface to pinch the ball against the grass to create the backspin, which is necessary to lift the ball into the air. The shortest club has the most loft.

Unfortunately, beginner golfers do just the opposite. They scoop under the ball with their hands in an attempt to lift the ball up into the air, instead of leading the club face through the ball with their arms and hands to let the clubhead do the work. The club does the work if you let it.

THE SHORT GAME

During eighteen holes of golf there may be several occasions when you will be between clubs. Not being able to rely on anything less than a full shot to the green is like trying to stop a car on ice. You don't have full control.

The short game is the equalizer in golf and it can be the most rewarding and the most fun part of the game. I don't care how far your golfing buddy hits the ball, if you're approach shot to the green was short, you can still get close to the hole for a par if you have a reliable short game. For example, If your chipping is good and you're a few yards off the green you definitely have a good chance of tying the hole or even making a birdie.

The more you practice your short game the better your full iron shots will be, because every time you practice a short shot you're training your arms and hands. Practice swinging the club while concentrating on your hands and left arm leading the clubface to sweep the grass in front of the ball after contact. This keeps the back of your left wrist straight as it moves through impact to prevent you from scooping up the ball with your hands. Trust your tempo or your hands may de-celerate.

Half shots or less

Practice swinging the club back and forth with enough momentum for the downswing to finish with the clubshaft parallel to the ground and the clubhead pointing at the target. Your wrists release at impact, but they don't hinge. Prior to your actual swing visualize where you want the clubhead and your hands to finish. Swing. Step off the distance from you to where the ball landed. Then you'll know from what distances to use this shot when approaching the green.

Three quarter shots

Practice swinging the clubhead back and forth with enough momentum for the downswing to finish with your arms above your waist, slightly above parallel to the ground, with your wrists hinged pointing the clubshaft almost straight up. Prior to your actual swing, visualize where your hands should finish and swing.

      Step off the distance.

Feeling the shot

Relax your wrists, don't consciously control the tempo, instead look at the target, then practice swinging the club with what you feel is enough momentum to get the ball to it. As soon as you can feel this tempo stay committed and trust it, set up to the ball, glance again at the target and swing. Practice to targets from various distances beginning from eighty yards in. This swing is really all about feel and trust. Practice builds confidence.

CHIPPING

If a golfer has difficulty chipping, it's a good bet he or she is experiencing problems with their full irons as well. If you want to become a proficient iron player, practice your chipping: When you practice chipping, you're training your wrists, hands and arms for all the clubs; chipping is really just a shortened swing. However, unlike your full swing, your head doesn't move after ball contact. The left hand must control the swing, the right hand supplies the energy at impact.

SETTING UP TO THE BALL

Set up to the ball; place the ball in the center of your stance or closer to your right foot if you want a lower ball flight. Your hands must be positioned ahead of the ball and remain ahead of it until after impact. Your right knee should remain relaxed to prevent tension, it may move slightly during impact, that's okay. Just as in a full swing, don't de-celerate your left arm or your right hand will turn the club over at impact.

Hands finish ahead of the ball

Place your hands forward of the ball and focus on slightly sweeping the grass in front of it. This is so important, I will repeat it: do not focus on the ball, instead focus on sweeping the grass in front of it. The ball has to move. The back of your left wrist must not break down as the club face sweeps the grass lightly and follows through to the target. After contact, your hands should still be ahead of the clubhead.

CHIPPING PRACTICE

Practice the chipping stroke without a ball with your pitching wedge, sweeping the grass through the impact zone until you can execute it reasonably well. Place the ball into the center of your feet or closer to the right foot if you want the ball fight to be lower, focus on sweeping the grass in front of the ball and following through to the target. Remember: the ball has to move forward, because the grass is in front of it. Chip balls to land approximately five feet in front of you.

Success is all about the back of your left wrist remaining straight as your left arm leads, and trusting your stroke and tempo. Practice to this distance until you can get within at least fifteen inches of the target. This may take some time, but you will get it.

The further the distance the shorter the club

You may think it should be the other way around, but it isn't, the longer clubs, five iron for example, can't stop as quickly as a pitching wedge from the same distance: the wedge has more braking power (back spin). Just keep in mind, the shorter the club the less distance the ball rolls after landing.

Between fifteen and five feet

Practice to distances between fifteen and five feet. Begin with your pitching wedge from fifteen feet and finish from five feet with your five iron. This chip is for when the flag is close to the edge of the green, the ball should land just on the edge of it and roll up to the hole.

Between thirty feet and fifteen feet

When the ball is further away from the edge of the green, you will use this shot to land the ball just on the green and roll up to the hole. Begin with your sandwedge then move forward approximately five feet and select the next longest club and so on, finishing up with your five iron from fifteen feet..

During actual play, you'll soon learn which club to use and when. With practice, you will able to chip the ball closer to the target than you can toss it. When you see a professional golfer chip the ball into the hole, you can be sure he or she has practiced a lot.

Good chipping relieves tension

It's impossible to over-emphasize the importance of practicing your chipping. If your approach shot misses the green, you'll still feel positive about the final outcome, because you'll know you can recover. Plus when you chip the ball to roll into the hole, it will usually land close enough to the pin for an easy one putt. Chances are also good that during the round you'll chip the ball into the hole for a birdie (one under).

After a long drive onto the fairway and missing your approach shot to the green, there's no worse feeling, if instead of recovering, you chip the ball thirty feet past the pin and two putt for a bogie (one over).

THE LOB SHOT

Unlike other swings: consciously hinge your wrists early in your backswing, and re-hinge them early in the downswing, the clubhead should point skyward.

Take a few practice swings first to feel the correct tempo for the distance to the green. The tempo is usually much slower than full shots. You'll have to do a few practice swings before you'll know how little or how much. Depending on the situation, select a sandwedge or a pitching

wedge. Once you've taken your practice swing and established what you believe to be the correct tempo, don't deviate from it during the actual shot. If you need a pitching wedge to get the ball over a bunker and stop quick. Place the ball between your heels, the left arm controls the club, keep your hands ahead of the ball and follow through.

There will be other occasions when you'll need a sandwedge because the ball trajectory must be higher than normal for the ball to land softly onto the green. Set up with the ball off your left heel or maybe slightly more forward depending on the trajectory for a particular shot. Open the clubface; you want to get the club under the ball, similar to playing out of sand. The ball must be sitting up on the grass with enough room for the opened clubface (above) to slide under the ball.

The low iron punch shot

You may have seen professional players hit low flying shots under trees. You can do it too. Place most of your weight onto your left foot, position the ball more inside your right foot than your left: the closer the ball is to it the lower the trajectory will be. Your hands will be well ahead of the ball because of its position. Take practice swings feeling for enough momentum to land the ball where you intend it to. Only practice will tell which club to use for a certain distance.

SAND SHOTS

Open the club face and position the ball off your left heel. At the top of your back-swing your hands should be fully hinged. Your right hand moves under your left hand during the downswing (in this particular situation). Keep the flange on the edge of the clubface open through impact to remove the sand from under the ball, to land it softly onto the green. The further the distance to the hole, the less sand to remove from under the ball. Practice removing various amounts of sand to learn how much to remove. A smooth backswing and follow through is a must. Practice builds confidence.

PUTTING

Set up comfortably to the ball with your feet and shoulders parallel to the putting line. Position your eyes directly over the ball. Hold your putter firmly on the line with your right hand, while you grip it with your left hand, then adjust your right hand grip. During practice, pay attention to the forward stroke to see where the putter head becomes perfectly square to the line: place the ball just into this area so that the putter face will be square to line at impact.

The backswing

Maintain a steady head as you stroke the ball by moving the putter with your shoulders; rocking your arms and hands back and through. Practice reading greens and selecting the line to the hole from all distances. Focus on stroking the ball smoothly through the contact area. Stay committed to your practice swing, your tempo and the line you selected. Trust is important, without it you may second guess your practice stroke and miss the putt.

The follow through

Practice putting mostly from ten feet. Many scoring opportunities are missed from this distance. You want to be confident you can get the ball into the hole for a par, or if your recovery chip is ten feet short, you can sink it for a par. If you've practiced your chipping, most of your recovery chips shouldn't be more than ten feet from the hole.

As a young beginning golfer, I practiced my irons and driver on a regular basis, but I paid little attention to my putter. That was until after I played in a two-day pro-am team tournament. My game was solid until my partners counted on me to make pressure putts. I missed the putts, not once, but many times. After the first day I was devastated. The second day I just couldn't wait to finish the round. I'm sure my partners couldn't wait either.

I learned my lesson. Practice your putting as much as any other part of the game. Half of the golf stokes are putting strokes.

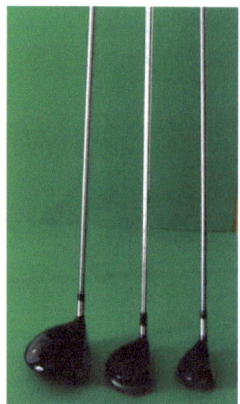

Driver, 3-wood and utility clubs

The new drivers are much easier to control than they were about ten years ago, but you still have to work hard to swing them. The difference between swinging a driver, the three wood and the utility club is your tempo: it's usually faster. You can swing the driver as fast as you wish as long you can maintain your balance and your swing is smooth.

      Establish your tempo during your practice swing: swing the driver until you can hear the swish; be certain to repeat this tempo during the actual shot. Remember, like all clubs, don't attempt to hit the ball: swing through it. Focus on where your hands are to finish.

PROBLEMS ON THE COURSE

Forget the bad shot, it's gone, there's nothing you can do to erase it. Plan your next shot. Take a practice swing. Trust it. Swing.

There will be times when you may make as many bad shots as good ones. Unless you are willing to accept the bad along with the good you will never enjoy this game. In the beginning, you decided that you would enjoy playing golf, "the greatest game in the world." It's important to remind yourself that from time to time.

No matter where the bad shot lands, the challenge is to get it back onto the fairway or onto the green. Did you ever stop and think about the word "fairway?" It means precisely what it implies, the fair way. The remainder of the course is made up of hazards.

This is the game, accept it; with acceptance comes enjoyment, with enjoyment comes enthusiasm, with enthusiasm comes a peaceful mind: a must for good golf.

Stretch before playing or practicing

I can't recall the number of times I've been on the practice range listening to a frustrated golfer complaining because his or her shoulders and hips won't turn completely or their legs aren't reacting in sink with the rest of their body. In other words, their body parts aren't working in sequence.

If you neglect to stretch your shoulders, arms, hips and legs before practicing or playing, your body won't be relaxed or responsive. This usually leads to a bad practice session and poor performance on the course for at least a few holes. Even worse, you may not find your best swing during the round.

Stretching only takes a few minutes and it may even prevent a muscle injury. Before playing, if you don't have enough time to both stretch and practice, skip the practice.

I learned this lesson the hard way. I had to meet a work deadline and arrived late at the golf course. I decided to skip the stretching, instead I went directly to the tee box. My golfing buddies were impatiently waiting for me, they had already teed off. I apologized, quickly teed up the ball and swung. Suddenly I felt some muscles in my chest pop. The ball landed fifty yards up the fairway. I couldn't even speak to tell my buddies what had just occurred. I left the ball on the fairway, waved goodbye and headed for the doctors office in great pain.

When I asked for a prescription, he said, "

take aspirins, no golf for a month and practice your putting, I've seen you putt, it's not good. Next time be sure to stretch." The doctor was right, I learned my lesson, the chest muscles eventually healed, and my putting improved.

Warm up without the ball first

After stretching, take a few minutes to practice swinging your five iron and driver. During your practice swing, sweep the grass and concentrate on your hips and legs moving. If you're short of time, spend less time on the practice range.

Don't keep score for five rounds

It's only natural for you to want to know how low you can score. However, I strongly recommend that you continue to practice your swing instead. If you attempt to score you may get too goal orientated and override your newly grooved swing. Pick the ball up off the green on every hole, don't try to score for at least the first five rounds. When you're playing with friends, just explain that you are grooving a new swing.

The practice swing first

Take a practice swing before every golf shot even if you contacted the last ball perfectly. One good practice swing is sufficient, listen for the swish.

If your practice swing wasn't correct, correct it before making the shot. This will take less time than it will for you to go looking for the ball in the woods later. Executing the actual shot after a bad practice swing usually results in a repeat of the bad swing. Relax your muscles and clear your mind: Take a few deep breaths and listen to your breathing for a few seconds; it's almost impossible to listen to your breathing and think anxious thoughts at the same time. Repeat your practice swing.

Once you're satisfied with your practice swing, don't consciously increase your tempo during your actual swing. If you do, you'll override the practice swing tempo. Not only will your actual swing be jerky, the results will be poor. Trust your swing.

Controlling your ego

Paul Flache, a professional hockey player, former student of mine and a good friend, consistently scores in the low seventies. I believe it's because of his professional hockey attitude. When his ball lands in a hazard he never complains, he actually loves the challenge of getting out of it. He believes he can get out of it and usually does.

I have another student whose swing is as good or better, but because of his attitude he can't break eighty. As soon as he has a bad hole he's toast, his ego gets in the way.

Egos, more than fairway hazards, can prevent you from shooting lower scores. Your ego (that other little voice in your head) wants to see your ball in a hazard or behind one. It enjoys warning you about all of them, especially when you're about ready to swing.

After you swing, if the results are bad, your ego will call you names you'd never say around your mother. It tries to intimidate you so you'll relinquish control to it. Sometimes you do. Even though, as the old saying goes, "it can talk it, but it can't walk it."

Your ego wants you to become even more anxious, so it continues to berate you as you walk down the fairway. It warns you about past errors and tells you that you aren't up to the task at hand. You wouldn't tolerate a loud mouth golfing partner who treated you like that, you'd know he or she was trying to throw you off your game. So is your ego.

The good news is you don't have to tolerate it. It's your choice. Don't talk back to it. Believe it or not, just like the loud mouth golfing partner, that's what your ego wants you to do. It knows arguing or complaining creates additional stress and detracts you from your task at hand. Stay in the present and go about your business. Deep breaths, take your practice swing, look at your target, concentrate on the finish and swing.

On thinking positive

My boys and I have won our fair share of skins and best ball tournaments over the years. But the game I recall the most happened a few years ago. We were a team of four playing in an 18 hole best ball charity.

We were about to tee off on the one hundred and ninety foot par three eighteenth, when suddenly the marshal walked onto the green. My son Luke yelled and asked what he was doing. He informed us he was removing the closest to hole flag, because he was sure we wouldn't get any closer than the three foot mark already established.

All three boys hollered simultaneously, "leave it in, one of us will get it closer." Now that's thinking positive. They all did, except for me, I was a bit short. My son Luke's ball was one foot from the hole. The marshal was our witness. When we turned in our scores we discovered we had also won the tournament by one stroke.

Focus where you want the ball to land

The power of suggestion, most of us have already experienced it. For example: sometimes when we're thinking don't drop that glass, don't spill it, be careful you could slip, etc, we do.

Once, while golfing with a low handicap senior golfer, I commented on all the hazards to the green we were playing. He replied, "what hazards I don't see them, I only see unobstructed air between my ball and the green, there's no trouble there."

He explained that of course he was aware of them, but once he's set up to the ball he only sees his target. "If you focus on the target you can't focus on the hazards," he said. Don't think about where you don't want your ball to go or that's just where it might end up.

Swing then go look for it

I loved to watch Arnold Palmer because he took calculated risks. Some say it cost him a few matches. I don't think so. I believe he won more than he would have had he been afraid to lose.

Don't be afraid to take calculated risks. Nothing creates tension more than the fear of losing. Remember, your real golfing friends won't judge you by your golf score, they'll judge you by your demeanor on the golf course. Afraid to lose, afraid to win: swing then go look for it.

Ignore your butterflies

No matter how confident you are with your golf swing, you are bound to get butterflies every once in a while. As a beginner, it may happen on the first tee, or as you become more experienced it may happen as you are about to shoot your best score ever. The Cure: focus on the target and take a few good practice swings. Trust your swing. Remember: it's okay to have butterflies as long as they fly in formation.

Practice creates confidence

If you don't bring a grooved swing to the golf course, you won't find one out there. Practice with every club in the bag as much as possible. Unfortunately many golfers practice more with the driver than all the other clubs in their bag combined. In most situations you can compensate for a missed drive much easier than you can make up for a missed approached shot. Confidence only comes from practicing with every club.

Practice your swing indoors and outdoors, with or without a ball. In the summer you can practice at a practice range or brush the grass in your backyard, or tee up a whiffle ball. In the winter you can sweep an old carpet, or maybe go to an indoor practice range.

TEACHING NOTES

Swinging over the top

A former student telephoned to tell me he couldn't stop swinging his arms and the club around over the top. I asked him if he was starting the club down with his left foot as he had been taught. He told me he was. I asked him if his head moved as his left side turned to move his arms and club back. He told me it was.

I told him even if his backswing felt correct his body must be moving up off the ball, either during his backswing or downswing, I told him to forget about golf balls for a while, instead to practice his full swing brushing the grass with his three wood in his backyard. To his surprise, he couldn't brush it. I told him practice this until he could.

A few days later he called to tell me his swing felt powerful and his iron shots were solid.

Skipping the practice swing

My student was flailing away at golf balls. When I asked her why she wasn't taking practice swings or waggling the club before swinging she didn't answer. I just stood quietly and watched. I'm sure she knew what I was thinking.

Finally she stopped and began taking practice swings. It wasn't long before her tempo improved. I tossed five balls to her. All five shots were absolutely perfect. I asked her what had made the difference. She replied, "My practice swing, my tempo and thinking of a complete finish, not the ball." Results good.

Not completing the shoulder turn.
I could see that she wasn't completing her backswing and was swinging around and over the top. I told her she was lifting the club with her arms instead of turning her left side (shoulders, hips, knees) to move her arms to the top of her backswing. She told me she couldn't turn her shoulders that far. I asked her to keep her arms relaxed, and to allow her head to move freely as she turned her left side. And to practice her downswing by sweeping the club through the grass in the impact area: this would help keep her knees slightly bent, and her legs moving. Results good.

Hitting at the ball
She's the fastest learner I've ever taught. Now she's scuffing the ball, and hitting weak shots along the ground. I told her the swing was okay, but she was trying to hit the ball too hard instead of swinging through it. She insisted there must be another problem. To convince her otherwise, I told her to take at least ten practice swings, while listening for her swing's swish sound and to picture her hands finishing at the top of her swing. I reminded her that this was her tempo, and if she couldn't hear a swish sound to swing the club until she could. Next I had her step up to the ball and swing. The results were good.

Stiff arms and too far from the ball
A student was struggling with his takeaway; his arms appeared stretched and stiff and he was off balance at the finish. I told him to position his club the correct distance from his body, his weight was mostly on his toes because he was setting up too far from the ball. I asked him to relax his arms, grip the club and to lift it up to parallel. Next, to let his arms and club drop down in front of him as far possible before bending forward, just far enough to sole the club's edge square to the target line. His takeaway is back on track.

Slowing to watch the ball

I was practicing at an out of town practice range, when I noticed this middle aged club member knocking balls in every direction. He kept glancing over at me with a look on his face that seemed to be saying "please help."

As he was passing by on his way back from getting another bucket of balls, he stopped to tell me that he just couldn't make his driver work. He said he was keeping his eyes on the ball, but he couldn't get a solid hit.

I told him that this wasn't his problem, to me it looked as if he was slowing his swing at impact. He was fixated on the ball like an anxious deer staring into headlights. I told him he's probably heard the words " don't move your head, watch the ball. It's bad advice, you must allow your head to move after impact."

I explained I wasn't telling him not to look at the ball, just not to stare at it. Instead to focus on maintaining his tempo through the ball all the way to the finish. I demonstrated the swish sound and told him he could establish his tempo by swinging the club while he listened for it; when he could hear it, to set up to the ball and swing.

I watched him practice for a few minutes, then I continued practicing. Later as I was about to head for home, the club's manager walked up to me and asked what I had told him. He said, " whatever it was it's working." He told me the gentleman had come into the club house to tell him his swing was fixed. The manager asked if he supplied the cart, would I take this fella to play a few holes. He went on to tell me this fella had never been able to get satisfactory results from his driver.

Hands closing the club face

His club face was closed at impact. I explained that during his downswing his hands would return the club to its original soled position. We reviewed the neutral grip and soling the club. I demonstrated how he should hold the club with his right hand as he places his left hand grip onto the club, and to hold the club steady with his left grip as he places his right grip onto the club. I helped him to place his hands in the neutral position, and told him to go ahead and swing. The results were good.

SWING CURES
1. Your grip is too tight.

Relax your arms, let them hang like a rope, grip the club lightly and lift it up with your arms and waggle it. Your hands should have secured the club; you should be able to feel the clubhead. Once you have soled the club, be careful not to increase the grip pressure with either hand.

2. Your arms are lifting the club

"Your left side should be moving your arms." Your shoulders, hips, and right knee (as a unit) turn and lift your passive arms to swing the club back to the top of your backswing. You'll never develop a reliable swing if it's only your hands and arms that are lifting the club.

3. The club is going outside.

You may be trying to move the club back in a straight line. Allow your left side to move the club back a short distance before it turns naturally inside the line, as it continues to follow along to the top of your backswing.

4. Your weight didn't move into your right leg.

You may be lifting your arms and the club straight up instead of turning your left side to swing the club back, or maybe your head is stuck: either situation would prevent your weight from transferring to your right foot. Keep your arms passive and turn your left side. Allow your head to subconsciously move along as your shoulders move. At the top of your backswing your head should be behind the ball.

5A. No downswing power

If your shoulders start the club down too soon, the powerful energy is lost before ball contact. Your left foot must be planted first to start the club down, just before you complete your backswing.

5B. No downswing power

There wasn't sufficient downswing power because your left side, especially your shoulders didn't complete the backswing, consequently most of your weight couldn't' shift to your left.

6. Can't get your body to swing in sequence
Practice focusing only on brushing the club back and through the grass. If you've practiced the three swing key moves correctly, brushing the grass definitely trains your body to swing in sequence, providing you don't consciously try to control it. Make certain that you finish your swing.

7A. The ball curves far right
You may be trying to take the club back on a straight line. You shouldn't because it will eventually go outside the line causing the ball to curve to the right. Allow your left side to move the club back in a straight line naturally, and then turn inside the target line, as it should.

7B. The ball curves far right or lacks power
You may be starting the club down by turning your hips first, instead of sliding them to your left before turning.

7C. The ball curves far right
You may be slowing to watch the ball.

8. The ball curves to the left

It's possible that you're lower body may be moving slightly slower than your upper body. Be sure to relax your lower body, especially your legs; plant your left foot first as you practice your overall swing tempo.

Trust your swing

Remember how natural and easy it was to dance with your newly discovered girlfriend or boyfriend, until you began thinking about your feet and where they should be going next; instead of looking into your new friends eyes and listening to the music. You lost your rhythm, your confidence and your legs became wooden. Maybe you even lost your new dancing partner. Your golf swing is no different. When you're on the course, if you begin thinking about all those moves your body parts have to make, you will lose your swing, your confidence, and golf will break your heart. Instead, listen for your swing's swish sound and swing, it's the music.

Keep notes after every round

When you experience a bad swing round be sure to document it. Later, after you've solved the problem, document the specific swing cure. Document the good rounds as well; explain what contributed most to your success. These notes will be invaluable to you because you'll be able to refer to them to solve recurring swing problems. Documenting my good and bad swings helped me to re-learn my swing and write this book.

FINAL WORDS
Finish your swing, forget the ball

If I could only give one tip to a new player I would tell him or her to finish the swing. Your goal is to swing the club correctly, not hit the ball. A smooth and complete swing launches the ball correctly.

I began playing golf when I was a kid, without any instruction. My weekly teachers were on "Shell's Wonderful World Of Golf". I would watch every episode and listen to every word the players and Gene Sarzen "the TV host" had to say.

I noticed some of the best player's hands finished high and were hinged. I didn't understand what they were doing at the time, but I began imitating their finished position, instead of trying to hit the ball. This was a big discovery for me. In fact, it was so easy to swing my driver, I felt as if I was cheating somehow. I'm sure most good golfers were very aware of the importance of swinging through the ball to finish their swing, instead of hitting away at a it, but to me it was an amazing discovery. I didn't understand what I was doing at the time, but I realize now that I was getting out of my body's way to allow it to swing freely. As long as I trusted it, my swing was good.

I still visualize my finish before swinging the club; including chipping. However, after re-learning my swing, my practice swing also consists of focusing on brushing the grass and keeping out of my body's own way: allowing it to swing the club without me consciously controlling all the necessary moves. This may sound easy to do and it is: it's only difficult when you don't trust your body to swing the club correctly. Learning to trust your swing may require some practice, but remember: trying fails, doing does, trust your body's swing.

As in life, play fair: play it were it lies.
Woodroe C. Nicholson

MY GOLF NOTES

MY GOLF NOTES

MY GOLF NOTES

MY GOLF NOTES

MY GOLF NOTES

www.ingramcontent.com/pod-product-compliance
Lightning Source LLC
Chambersburg PA
CBHW042309150426
43198CB00001B/18